AF399827

THE MAYFLOWER

The Founding Myth of the United States of America

Written by Marine Libert
In collaboration with Christelle Klein-Scholz
Translated by Emma Hanna

History 50MINUTES.com

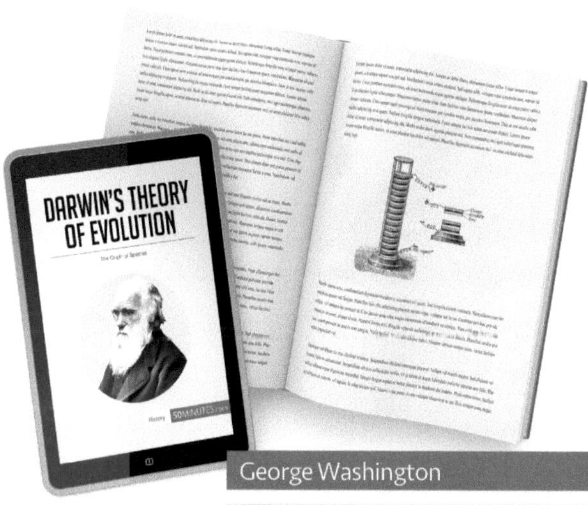

THE *MAYFLOWER*

KEY INFORMATION

- **When:** September to November 1620.
- **Where:** from Plymouth (England) to Plymouth (North America), via present-day Provincetown, Cape Cod.
- **Context:**
  - The European wars of religion (1524-1648) were raging across the continent.
  - King James I of Great Britain and Ireland (1566-1625) was taking action to suppress the activity of Puritan separatists, a Calvinist Protestant minority that sought to secede from the Church of England.
  - The first permanent British colonies were being established in North America.
- **Key protagonists:**
  - The Pilgrim Fathers, a group of Puritans whose beliefs conflicted with the teachings of the Church of England and who therefore wanted to secede from it and create a society where they could live according to their own

religious beliefs.
  - Non-Puritan or non-separatist English citizens with no real religious convictions who were nevertheless looking for a fresh start.
  - The Wampanoag, the Native American civilisation living in the region the Pilgrims settled in.
- **Impact:**
  - The colonisation of New England.
  - The outbreak of the American Indian Wars.
  - The creation of the founding myth of the United States of America.

INTRODUCTION

During the 16th and 17th centuries, Europe was engulfed in a series of conflicts driven by religious dissent. The Protestant Reformation, which was started by the German theologian Martin Luther (1483-1546) in 1517, challenged the legitimacy of the power wielded by the Pope and the clerical hierarchy of the Catholic Church. This led to a schism between the Roman Catholic Church and the Protestant Church which sent shockwaves through the political landscape of Europe, and several heads of state seized this opportunity to throw off the shackles of papal authority. For example, in 1534, King Henry VIII of England (1491-1547) founded the Church of England, a Protestant church that was to be governed directly by the King himself – in other words, without papal intervention. Although this new state religion was abolished during the reign of his daughter Queen Mary I (1516-1558), it was re-established and consolidated by her half-sister and successor Queen Elizabeth I (1533-1603) and the monarchs who succeeded her. Following a period of religious uncertainty, Anglicanism (the doctrine preached by the Church of England) emerged as the dominant religion in Great Britain, and any deviation from its teachings was banned.

The prevailing climate of religious repression in England at this time led 102 migrants, the majority of whom were Puritans who disagreed with the teachings of the Church of England, to board a ship called the *Mayflower* at Plymouth harbour in 1620 and set sail for the uncharted lands of North America in order to forge a new life there. Although the voyage promised to be long and fraught with danger, the prospect of being able to openly practise their religion proved sufficient motivation for them to take their chances. These travellers set a precedent that paved the way for countless other British colonists to cross the Atlantic, and their story was immortalised for generations to come as the founding myth of the United States of America.

POLITICAL, SOCIAL AND RELIGIOUS CONTEXT

RELIGIOUS PERSECUTION IN ENGLAND

When Mary Tudor was crowned Queen of England in 1553, she attempted to abolish the Church of England that had been founded by her father Henry VIII. She was the only surviving child from her father's marriage to his first wife, the Spanish princess Catherine of Aragon (1485-1536). Like her mother, Mary I was a devout Catholic, and her determination to restore the Catholic Church in England resulted in the ruthless persecution of Protestants throughout the country. In fact, Mary went as far as to sentence 284 people to death, generally by being burned at the stake, which earned her the nickname "Bloody Mary". When she died in 1558, she was succeeded by her younger half-sister Elizabeth I, who restored Anglicanism as the state religion.

ANGLICANISM VS. PURITANISM

Elizabeth I was a pragmatic ruler whose main goal was to ensure national unity. To that end, her religious policy was based on compromise: she advocated a branch of Anglicanism that was, essentially, a balanced combination of Catholic and Protestant beliefs. However, this compromise satisfied neither the Catholics, who believed in the supremacy of papal authority, nor the Protestants, who wanted to implement much more sweeping reforms within the Church. In sum, the Protestants – particularly Calvinists – wanted to strip the Church down to its essence, distancing it from the pomp and fanfare associated with the Catholic Church and returning instead to the faith's humble origins. They also rejected the hierarchical structure of the Catholic Church, and objected particularly strongly to the role of bishops. Because of this desire to "purify" the Anglican Church, they came to be known as "Puritans". They also believed that the only legitimate system of church governance was congregationalism, whereby each local church congregation is independent, founded by members of the congregation itself, and led by a university-educated pastor who is chosen by the congregation and can be dismissed by them at any time. The Puritans argued that the legitimacy of this system of governance was supported by Biblical teachings, but Queen Elizabeth viewed the fact that they refused to recognise any religious authority aside from their own pastor as an unacceptable threat to her own position as head of the Church of England.

DID YOU KNOW?

A congregation can be defined as a group of people who share the same religious convictions and values.

During the first centuries of the Common Era – the period when the Christian faith was established and the gospels were written – the congregation was upheld as an institution of pivotal importance due to the simple fact that it was not part of a centralised organisation: the head of the congregation was the highest authority it answered to. Furthermore, the teachings of Jesus regarding this subject have been interpreted in a variety of ways, giving rise to numerous theological disputes. For example, the clerical hierarchy that was created in the 4th century, which still forms an integral part of the Catholic Church today, is viewed as unbiblical by Protestants and was one of the main issues at stake during the Reformation in the 16th century.

The coronation of James I (1566-1625) as King of England in 1603 was welcomed enthusiastically by the Puritans. Given that the new King had previously been crowned King James VI of Scotland in 1567, they hoped that the principles of the Church of Scotland, which were based on Calvinism, would soon be extended to England. However, these hopes were soon crushed: the newly-crowned King adopted Elizabethan Anglicanism and reaffirmed the role of bishops during a meeting with Puritan leaders in 1604 by proclaiming "No bishop, no king" (Barlow: 1804, p. 27). By doing so, he founded his authority on the principle of divine right, which states that his right to rule is conferred by God and that the bishops' duty is to provide him with guidance during his reign.

The Scottish Reformation

The Church of Scotland is governed by a Calvinist polity known as Presbyterianism. This system involves church governance being managed by the communities themselves at a local level, while also answering to a national or regional assembly. This alternative organisational structure replaces the traditional Catholic hierarchy with a number of national and local levels of power.

In fact, religious dissenters faced even harsher political oppression under the reign of James I than they had during the Elizabethan era. This was largely because the king believed that underground religious meetings were a breeding ground for conspiracies against the Crown, and he therefore had a number of influential pastors arrested. This created further divisions in the Puritan ranks, as certain factions still hoped to eradicate all Catholic influence from the Anglican Church, while others were convinced that any attempt to do so would be futile, and that the only viable solution was to split off from the Church of England entirely. Because of this conviction, they were generally known as "separatists". As time went by, the idea of leaving England's shores for good and settling somewhere far away, where they could practise their religion freely, became more and more attractive to the separatists.

FLEEING TO THE NETHERLANDS

In 1607, a congregation of separatist Puritans from the village of Scrooby in Nottinghamshire decided to flee England for good, even though it was forbidden to leave the country without authorisation. Their first escape attempt failed, but in 1608 the Scrooby congregation successfully fled the country and settled in the Dutch town of Leiden.

In those days, Leiden was a university city where personal and intellectual freedom was protected by law, which meant that large numbers of Puritans had flocked there. The newly-arrived separatists from the English countryside had to struggle to adapt to this unfamiliar urban environment and lifestyle; being foreigners, many were left with no choice but to take on exhausting jobs in the textile industry. They gradually realised that they were now exiles, as described by the English separatist William Bradford (1590-1657) in his chronicles: "They knew they were Pilgrims" (Bradford: 1952, p. 33).

Prior to the 16th century, the Dutch Republic, which comprised a number of provinces located in the present-day Netherlands, was controlled by the Kingdom of Spain, which at that time was ruled by King Philip II (1527-1598). However, the region revolted against Spanish rule and declared independence in 1568, which led to the Eighty Years' War (1568-1648).

There were many motivating factors that influenced this conflict, including a religious dimension, as the Dutch Republic was largely Protestant, whereas the Spanish monarch was a devout Catholic. Nevertheless, the two sides signed what was known as the Twelve Years' Truce in Antwerp in 1609, which led to a period of great prosperity throughout the region as many Protestants from all over Europe flocked there.

As the truce between Catholic Spain and the Dutch Republic was drawing to an end and hostilities looked set to resume, the Puritans living in Leiden began to fear that Spanish forces would seize control of the city. As such, they decided to leave, and received permission from the English government and funding from the Virginia Company to found a colony in North America. The English government's motives were simple: compared with the potential income a new colony could generate, the colonists' religious beliefs were of little consequence. The government therefore gave the would-be colonists a license that granted them permission to establish a settlement at the mouth of the Hudson River, and the Puritan congregation took passage back to England on a merchant ship called the *Speedwell*. When they arrived, a second vessel that had been prepared for the journey across the Atlantic was waiting for them: the *Mayflower*.

| *The* Mayflower *in Plymouth Harbor*, by William Formby Halsall, 1882.

JOURNEY TO THE NEW WORLD

Those who wanted to start a new life in America had to contend with a multitude of dangers. It was not simply a matter of surviving the Atlantic crossing: the true challenge lay in adapting to the new life that awaited prospective colonists in the uncharted lands on the other side of the ocean. Furthermore, England was awash with horror stories about the fate of the first English colonists who had been sent to America. In fact, the inhabitants of Roanoke (an island off the coast of present-day North Carolina) are still commonly known as the "lost colony" due to the fact that they disappeared without a trace, while the inhabitants of the Jamestown colony in Virginia were decimated by famine, illness and clashes with the native population. Failures notwithstanding, the first colonists had still been well-prepared for their task, and the Puritans emulated them by recruiting men with the skills that were deemed necessary to build a new society, such as carpenters and blacksmiths. These individuals were generally non-separatist Puritans or Anglicans, but most of the new re-cruits actually had no firm religious convictions. However, even though the Pilgrims called them "strangers", they all shared one common goal: to make a fresh start.

DID YOU KNOW?

The Jamestown colony was founded by Captain John Smith (c. 1579-1631), who is best known for his association with Pocahontas (c. 1596-1617), the daughter of the chief of the Powhatan Confederacy. In 1607, Smith was reported to have been cap-tured by this tribe and saved by Pocahontas, who was aged 12 at the time. Following this episode, the two became friends. Smith later returned to England in 1609 after being injured by a gunpowder explosion.

Pocahontas saving John Smith's life, c. 1870

The initial plan for the Atlantic crossing was to send two ships: the *Mayflower* and the *Speedwell*. However, the *Speedwell* had problems with a leak in the hull, and had to remain in Plymouth harbour. This misfortune was compounded when strong winds further delayed the ship's departure, and the passengers were stuck on board throughout this time, forcing them to consume some of their provisions before the start of the voyage. In the end, the *Mayflower* did not set sail until 6 September.

KEY PROTAGONISTS

THE PILGRIMS FROM THE SCROOBY CONGREGATION

William Brewster (c. 1566-1644)

William Brewster was born into a well-off family living in Scrooby, near Doncaster, in 1568. He briefly studied at Cambridge before entering the service of William Davison (1541-1608), who served as Secretary of State under Elizabeth I, in 1584. However, his diplomatic career was cut short when his mentor was disgraced, arrested and imprisoned. He then returned to Scrooby, where he became postmaster and held regular secret meetings of the Puritan congregation in his manor house.

Brewster was the only one of the *Mayflower* Pilgrims who had prior political and diplomatic experience. He was also the highest-ranking member of the congregation who was not a member of the clergy, which resulted in him quickly becoming one of the community's leaders.

During the congregation's time in Leiden, he took advantage of the freedom of expression there to print a large number of tracts criticising James I's policies and Anglican beliefs. The King was furious, and even sent men to the Netherlands in search of him.

This meant that when the time came to start actively preparing for the journey across the Atlantic, Brewster was forced to go into hiding. This came as a tremendous blow to the rest of the congregation, who had been expecting to rely on his political experience during the negotiations with the authorities in London. However, Brewster managed to rejoin the other passengers of the *Mayflower* in Southampton just before the ship's grand departure in 1620.

In Plymouth, Massachusetts, he was the oldest member of the group, and acted as an advisor to Governor William Bradford. He died in April 1644 and was buried in the local graveyard.

John Carver (before 1584-1621)

Very little is known about the life of John Carver prior to his marriage to Katherine White, one of the members of the Puritan separatist congregation, in Leiden. From this point onwards, he began forging strong connections with the leading members of the congregation, notably with the pastor John Robinson (1575-1625), and was made a deacon. After Brewster was forced to go into hiding in order to evade the men sent after him by James I, it was left to Carver to negotiate with the English government. This won him great respect within the congregation, and he was elected governor of the new colony after their arrival in America.

In April 1621, he began suffering from a terrible headache and severe back pains one evening after work, and fell into a coma shortly afterwards. He never recovered, and his wife succumbed to the same disease five weeks later. Both had been badly weakened after a bout of illness they had suffered in January.

William Bradford (1590-1657)

William Bradford was born into a wealthy farming family in Austerfield, Yorkshire in 1590. By the age of 12, he had lost his parents, sister and grandfather and was taken in by his uncles. He was a sickly child who was unable to work in the fields and spent a great deal of time reading. As a result, he developed strong religious convictions which led him to leave Austerfield in search of a community that shared his personal beliefs, and eventually found it in the form of the Scrooby congregation.

After the death of John Carver in the spring of 1621, he was elected the second governor of the Plymouth colony. He was re-elected 30 times, and held the post until 1656. He also penned a journal that covered the first 30 years of the Plymouth colony's existence, which was later published as *Of Plymouth Plantation*.

He died in 1657 and was buried in the graveyard in Plymouth. The inscription on his gravestone reads: "Qua patres difficillime adepti sunt nolite turpiter relinquere" ("What our forefathers with so much difficulty secured, do not basely relinquish").

John Robinson (1575-1625)

John Robinson was born in Sturton-Le-Steeple, Nottinghamshire in 1576, and studied at Corpus

Christi College at the University of Cambridge. He became a pastor and moved to Norwich with his wife, where he clashed with the town's bishop due to their differing interpretations of church doctrine, and was suspended from his position. He returned to Sturton-Le-Steeple and became friends with William Brewster, whose beliefs were aligned with his own. He then became the assistant pastor of the Scrooby congregation.

He did not sail for America on the *Mayflower*, choosing instead to remain in the Dutch Republic to look after the members of the congregation who had been forced to abandon the voyage when the *Speedwell* was deemed unseaworthy. Although he had hoped to join the colony at a later date, he died in Leiden on 1 March 1625.

THE "STRANGERS"

Christopher Martin (1582-1621)

Christopher Martin was the governor of the *Speedwell*, and soon clashed with the Puritans. He consistently refused to cooperate with the Pilgrims while preparing for the voyage, preferring to work alone. Nevertheless, he was made governor of the *Mayflower* after the *Speedwell* was declared unseaworthy, and held the position until he was replaced by John Carver after their arrival.

He died in 1621 during a particularly harsh winter.

Christopher Jones (1570-1622)

Christopher Jones was born in 1570, and by 1620 he had already been Captain of the *Mayflower* for 11 years. Before setting sail for America, he had transported French wine to England and English wool to France. His crew for the Pilgrims' voyage across the Atlantic included two men who had already made the crossing: his First Mate, Robert Coppin, and his Pilot, John Clark (1573-1623).

Once the Pilgrims had been settled in the new colony, he returned to England and made another voyage to France. He died on the return trip in March 1622.

THE NATIVE AMERICANS

Massasoit (c. 1580-1662)

Massasoit was the chief of the Wampanoag tribe, an indigenous civilisation that lived in the Massachusetts Bay area where the passengers of the *Mayflower* landed. He brokered an alliance between his tribe and the Pilgrims that played a crucial role in helping the settlers to adapt to the unfamiliar land, notably because the Wampanoag showed them how to grow corn. In return, the Pilgrims offered him martial support against other Native American tribes.

He died in unknown circumstances between 1660 and 1662. He was succeeded by his son Wamsutta (also known as Alexander), who died shortly afterwards. His younger brother Metacomet (also known as Philip) then came to power.

| Massasoit and John Carver smoking a peace pipe.

THE *MAYFLOWER*

THE CROSSING

Although the Pilgrims had initially hoped that the entire congregation at Leiden would be able to make the crossing, many of them eventually abandoned the enterprise. Some were motivated by fear, others by fatigue, and some were simply left without a berth after the *Speedwell* was deemed unseaworthy. As a result, the group that eventually made the crossing was only half as large as expected.

It did not take long for conflict to break out during the voyage. The Pilgrims' radical religious views, ascetic lifestyle and the fact that they considered themselves models of virtue, which gave them a condescending air, did not endear them to the "strangers" they were travelling with. Knowing that the voyage would entail a variety of difficulties, Pastor John Robinson wrote a letter to his flock, encouraging them to "store up, therefore, patience against that evil day, without which we take offense at the Lord himself in his holy and just works" (Bradford: 1981, p. 57). This quote is a good illustration of the Puritan mindset, particularly the way they considered all of the trials they faced to be the will of God. This meant that they had to consider their clashes with the "strangers" and the sailors' jibes about their seasickness to be tests of faith like any other.

They lived in extremely rudimentary conditions on the ship. During bad weather, the passengers were no longer allowed on deck. Due to overcrowding and the lack of fresh air, the area below decks was quickly permeated with foul odours during these times, which made it difficult to breathe. They also had insufficient provisions, and the lack of vitamins in their diet led to scurvy. But although the travellers were getting weaker and weaker, their ordeal was not over yet: the ship was blown off course by a storm, and instead of reaching the mouth of the Hudson River, they arrived on the coast of Cape Cod. After attempting to turn south for their intended destination and almost running the ship aground on a reef, Captain Jones decided to remain at Cape Cod.

THE MAYFLOWER COMPACT

The preparations for making landfall did not go without incident. A group of agitators formed and demanded to be given their freedom once they landed, declaring that they would no longer answer to any form of authority. For most of them, the idea of living in a community governed by religious radicals was unbearable, but a number of them were also aware that the best way of ensuring the success of the venture was to remain unified in the face of adversity, and this attitude proved sufficient to quell the stirrings of unrest. However, this episode demonstrated the need for some kind of agreement between the different groups of travellers, and thus the Mayflower Compact was born.

The Compact is one of the cornerstones of the founding myth of the United States of America because, in the country's collective imagination, it is one of the texts that established American democracy. Although the Pilgrim Fathers had lived in a theocratic bubble until that point, they agreed to keep legal and religious matters separate from that point forward. This was partially because their time in the Dutch Republic had given them an appreciation of the benefits of a society that enforced separation of church and state, and partially because the number of "strangers" living among them left them powerless to do otherwise. In this document, they swore to respect the "just and equal Laws" (p. 84) that would be enacted by a provisional government known as a Civil Body Politic. However, the only religious practices permitted in the settlement would be those dictated by the Puritans.

Before they set foot on land, every able-bodied man signed the Compact, or drew a cross if they were illiterate. The colonists' next step was to elect a leader via a democratic vote, replacing Christopher Martin, who had filled this role during the voyage. The vote was divided among the "strangers", but the Pilgrims voted for John Carver *en masse*, which led to him being elected governor in Martin's place.

On 15 November 1620, the passengers of the Mayflower made landfall on American soil. After spending a few days freshening up and repairing the rowboat, they organised an expedition inland to find a source of fresh water where they could establish a settlement.

| *Signing of the Mayflower Compact, 1620,* by Edward Percy Moran, c. 1900.

FIRST CONTACT WITH THE WAMPANOAG

The settlers found traces of human habitation, including graves, abandoned huts and grain stores, as early as that first expedition inland. However, they did not encounter any people. The colonists therefore decided to appropriate the grain and a few other objects they had found, which earned them the natives' immediate distrust. Further expeditions were organised until one of them finally resulted in an encounter with the native population. It was not a peaceful affair: a shower of arrows rained down on the colonists, who responded with musket fire.

The settlers continued searching for a suitable location to establish a permanent settlement, and on 20 December 1620 they chose a site located two kilometres from Plymouth Rock, at the end of Long Beach. The first winter they spent there was extremely harsh, and the already-weakened travellers were plagued by colds, fevers and even scurvy. Worse still, their provisions were running low and the village's first houses were very crudely constructed, which meant that a significant proportion of the group lost their lives in February and March.

Furthermore, the Pilgrims constantly felt the eyes of the native population upon them, and lived in fear that an attack was imminent. One day, a Native American decided to venture into the settlement. According to Bradford's account, he showed no fear even though his arrival had thrown the camp into panic, and when his path was blocked by one of the colonists, he said "Welcome" (Young: 1841, p. 182), to the great surprise of all those present.

OFFICIAL MEETING AND ALLIANCE

The colonists were impressed, and offered the young man, who was named Samoset (c. 1590-1653), some food, drink and shelter – because, to the settlers' astonishment, he was almost completely naked despite the glacial wind that was blowing. It transpired that he was not from that region, but from Pemaquid Point in present-day Maine, and he had learned some basic English from the Europeans who fished in that area. He told the colonists that the area they were hoping to live in had once been prosperous, well-cultivated and heavily populated, but the population had recently been decimated by illness.

DEADLY DISEASES

The diseases that had ravaged the native population a few years before the *Mayflower* landed had been spread by the English sailors who fished the seas near

Maine. These illnesses, which included flu, measles, mumps and tuberculosis, were generally harmless for the Europeans, but were deadly to the indigenous population, as they had never been exposed to them before and therefore had never had the chance to build up immunity to them. The Pilgrims interpreted this tragedy as a sign of divine intervention, whereby the "promised land" had been deserted specifically so that they would be able to settle there.

Five days after his first visit, Samoset returned to announce that the Wampanoag chief, Massasoit, had come to meet the Pilgrims. His initial hostility to the colonists had been motivated by wariness after some of his men had been massacred by passing English sailors a few years earlier, but after watching the new arrivals, Massasoit had come to the conclusion that they were different: they seemed less aggressive, were accompanied by women and children, and were clearly trying to establish a permanent settlement. However, he had other motives for accepting the colonists' presence in his territory: although his people's numbers had been decimated by disease, the neighbouring Narragansett tribe had been unaffected and represented an increasing threat. Massasoit was therefore interested in the possibility of establishing a tactical alliance with the colonists, so the Wampanoag taught them how to grow corn and store it for the following winter in exchange for the promise of military support from the colonists. This alliance paid dividends a few months later when Massasoit was kidnapped by his rivals, and the English came to his rescue.

THE ORIGINS OF THANKSGIVING

Shortly after this episode, the Plymouth colonists invited Massasoit and his men to a meal in the village. It was harvest season, and the colonists' food stores were overflowing with corn, barley, pumpkins, beans and peas, so Bradford proclaimed that the following three days would be a special celebration that would henceforth be known as Thanksgiving.

Historically, Christians have held similar thanksgiving celebrations to thank God for all the good things that have come their way throughout the year through prayers and festivities. Bradford's Thanksgiving is also somewhat reminiscent of traditional English harvest festivals, when villagers gather to celebrate the end of summer. On this occasion, the Pilgrims were joined by Massasoit and one hundred of his warriors, who arrived at the settlement with five freshly slaughtered deer.

That day became a symbol of the unity of the American society of the future, and is still celebrated today. Every year on the fourth Thursday of November, Americans prepare a special meal consisting of a roast turkey and a pumpkin pie in memory of the meal the Pilgrims ate in the autumn of 1621. The story of Thanksgiving has been told, retold and embellished to such an extent that it has passed into legend, and it now forms an integral part of the history of the United States.

Did you know?

During the 17th and 18th centuries, Thanksgiving was not celebrated on an annual basis. It was Abraham Lincoln (American president, 1809-1865) who established the fourth Thursday of November as the official date of Thanksgiving in 1863.

At that time, the country was being ravaged by the American Civil War (1861-1865), and Lincoln saw Thanksgiving as a chance to bring the whole country together, no matter how divided they were at that moment, through an official holiday that celebrated their shared history. However, in the 20th century, criticism of the mystique surrounding the holiday became increasingly widespread, with its detractors pointing out that it presents a revisionist account of the relations between the first colonists and the indigenous population and erases all European culpability from the historical narrative.

IMPACT

NEW COLONIES

The Pilgrim Fathers paved the way for a number of other colonists who were also fleeing religious persecution in Europe. In November 1621, around 12 months after the *Mayflower*'s arrival, another ship brought 36 more colonists to Plymouth, including a number of other members of the Leiden congregation, and the colony began to thrive.

In 1630, Charles I (King of Great Britain and Ireland, 1600-1649) granted permission for John Winthrop (1588-1649) to establish and govern the Massachusetts Bay Colony. Once again, a local government consisting of a mixture of freemen and Puritans was established, and in 1691 the Plymouth colony was annexed by Massachusetts. Meanwhile, in 1624 a Dutch colony called New Amsterdam was founded at the mouth of the Hudson River, where the Pilgrims had originally intended to land. 40 years later, the English captured New Amsterdam and renamed it New York, in honour of the future King James II (1633-1701), who at that time was styled the Duke of York and was the brother of the reigning King Charles II (1630-1685). Several other colonies were also captured from the Dutch in the following years, notably the colony of Delaware, which had originally been founded by Swedish settlers in 1638.

The early years of the colonial era coincided with the rise of many radical religious sects influenced by the Protestant Reformation, including Separatists, Antinomians, Anabaptists, Millennialists, and Quakers. Members of each of these sects began arriving in America, and the Puritans of Massachusetts proved extremely intolerant when confronted with these alternative religious beliefs: for example, the Quaker Mary Dyer (c. 1611-1660) was hanged for her religious convictions.

| Mary Dyer being taken to the Boston Common
to be hanged.

The founder of the Rhode Island colony, Roger Williams (North American theologian and pastor, 1603-1683), had several serious disagreements with the Massachusetts-based pastor John Cotton (1584-1652). This conflict was because Williams' colony supported freedom of religion and advocated greater separation of church and state, arguing that the Puritans of Massachusetts did not truly respect this principle. As a result, the members of non-orthodox branches of Protestantism flocked to Williams' colony to seek refuge there, as did a large number of Jews. Thomas Hooker (Puritan leader, 1586-1647) also had a number of disputes with John Cotton, and eventually left to found the colony of Connecticut. Meanwhile, the colony of Maryland, which was founded by Cecilius Calvert (1605-1675) and his family in 1632, became known for welcoming the minority of Catholic English immigrants. In the following decades, the second generation of settlers began founding new colonies, including North Carolina (1653), South Carolina (1663), New Jersey (1664), Pennsylvania (1682) and Georgia (1733).

These thirteen English colonies thrived until 1776, when they became the United States of America with the signing of the Declaration of Independence.

KING PHILIP'S WAR

When the *Mayflower* landed in New England, this also marked the beginning of a series of conflicts known as the American Indian Wars, which pitted the colonists, and later the government of the United States of America, against the Native American tribes. Specifically, the conflict between the colonists at Plymouth and the Native Americans in that region came to be known as King Philip's War.

| *Philip, King of Mount Hope*, by Paul Revere, 1772.

When Massasoit died in 1662, his son Metacomet (c. 1639-1676), who was also known as King Philip, became the *sachem* ("chief") of the Wampanoag people. At that time, the Wampanoag's relations with the Europeans were deteriorating because of the massive influx of English immigrants who were settling on their lands. The colonists often took advantage of the fact that the Native Americans had no concept of private property to purchase large swathes of their territory for a paltry sum. There was also a shocking degree of inequality between the two civilisations: for example, the same crime was punished by a different sentence depending on who had committed it. In this way, a colonist could murder a Native American and face no reprisals from the colonial authorities, whereas a Native American who killed a European settler was likely to face a death sentence.

Eventually, Metacomet resolved to drive the colonists off his lands, but he knew that he did not have sufficient military strength to do so. He therefore began reaching out to other tribes in secret in an attempt to rally them to his cause, and the neighbouring French colonies in Acadia also provided him with a substantial supply of weapons. Events were irreversibly set in motion in 1675, when John Sassamon, a Native American who had converted to Christianity and acted as an informant for the English, was murdered. Following a show trial, three Wampanoag men were convicted of his murder and hanged, and it was commonly believed that they had acted on Metacomet's orders. These events sparked a revolt, and the settlement of Swansea in Massachusetts was attacked in June of that year. This was the first of a series of bloody raids.

Metacomet won several early victories, which convinced the Narragansett and Nipmuc tribes to ally themselves with the Wampanoag. However, the English regained the upper hand in December 1675 when they decimated Metacomet's Narragansett allies during the Great Swamp Fight. The Wampanoag suffered two further crushing defeats in the following months and were forced to flee towards Iroquois territory, losing the last of their allies in the process. However, the Iroquois had allied themselves with the English, and launched an attack of their own on Metacomet and his men. Soon afterwards, the *sachem* was betrayed by one of his warriors, captured and killed. By the time the war ended, it had taken a devastating toll on the Native American population: casualties are estimated at around 3000 Native Americans, compared to only 800 colonists.

THREATS TO THE NATIVE AMERICAN POPULATION

The colonies were the source of innumerable hardships faced by the Native American population in the following centuries. Although they had collectively numbered between 9 and 11 million at the end of the 15th century, there were only 250 000 Native Americans living in the United States by 1890. Large sections of the population were wiped out by epidemics, but famine was another leading cause of this decline, as bison were hunted almost to extinction and indigenous farmland was largely appropriated by the colonists.

Wherever the colonists settled, the native population only had two choices: they could assimilate and convert to the colonists' religion, or leave the area, which often meant abandoning the flora and fauna they held sacred. In other words, the colonisation of America amounted to a mass ethnocide of the Native American population, which culminated with the creation of Indian reservations in the 19th century and the US government forcibly confining the Native American population to those lands. This means that while many Americans consider Thanksgiving a celebration of their country's origins, many others view it as a way of misrepresenting and obscuring one of the darkest sides of the country's past.

SUMMARY

- The colonists who crossed the Atlantic Ocean aboard the *Mayflower* were separatist English Puritans who were fleeing religious persecution under King James I. They had previously sought refuge in Leiden, a city in the largely Protestant Dutch Republic, where the law permitted freedom of religion.
- They left Leiden because of renewed hostilities between the Dutch Republic and Spain, as well as a certain desire to maintain some connection to their homeland. The Pilgrims, as they would later come to be known, therefore decided to negotiate with the English government, and secured permission to found a colony, as well as funding from the Virginia Company.
- The Pilgrims were not the only ones to make the voyage: they were accompanied by tradesmen who had no separatist convictions, but whose skills would be necessary to build a settlement.
- They set sail from Plymouth harbour, England,

in early September 1620. In that era it was rare to attempt the voyage so late in the season, but the Pilgrims did not wish to delay any longer.

- The crossing took 65 days, which was ample time for friction to develop between the Puritans and the other passengers, whom they dubbed "strangers". Upon their arrival, they signed the Mayflower Compact to quell the tensions between the two factions and ensure that they would be able to coexist peacefully.
- They eventually dropped anchor in an area they named Plymouth, after the port they had sailed from. This was much further north than their planned destination.
- The land the colonists settled on was the ancestral territory of the Wampanoag people. However, their civilisation had been severely weakened by a deadly epidemic that had struck them three years earlier, killing thousands.
- In light of their weakened position and the increasing threat posed by the Narraganset, a rival tribe, the leader of the Wampanoag, a man named Massasoit, agreed to form an alliance with the colonists, who provided them with military aid in exchange for the Wampanoag's

advice and help in establishing a viable colony.

- As Plymouth began to thrive, other settlements began to spring up all along the Atlantic coast, which was a cause of increasing concern for the Native American population. Massasoit's son, who by that time had succeeded his father as leader, decided to try to put an end to colonialism in America by declaring war on the settlers, but this led to a crushing defeat for the Native American tribes who supported him.

We want to hear from you!
Leave a comment on your online library
and share your favourite books on social media!

FURTHER READING

BIBLIOGRAPHY

- Barlow, W. (1804) *The Summe of the Substance and the Conference which it Pleased His Excellent Majestie to Have with the Lords Bishops and Others of his Clergie (at which the Most of the Lords of the Council Were Present) in His Majesties Privie-Chamber, at Hampton Court, Jan. 14 1603*. London: Bye and Law Printers.

- Bradford, W. (1981) *Of Plymouth Plantation (1620-1647)*. New York: Modern Library College Editions.

- Dorel, F. (2006) La thèse du génocide indien : la guerre de position entre science et mémoire. *Amnis, revue de civilisation contemporaine Europes/Amériques*. [Online]. Issue 6. [Accessed 24 January 2018]. Available from: <http://journals.openedition.org/amnis/908>

- Martin, J-P. (1989) *Le puritanisme américain en Nouvelle Angleterre (1620-1693)*. Bordeaux: Presses universitaires de Bordeaux.

- Philbrick, N. (2006) *Mayflower: A Story of Courage, Community and War*. New York: Penguin Group.

- Young, A. (1841) *Chronicles of the Pilgrim Fathers of the Colony of Plymouth.* Boston: C.C. Little and J. Brown.

FILMS AND DOCUMENTARIES

- *Mayflower: The Pilgrims' Adventure.* (1979) [Film]. George Schaefer. Dir. USA: CBS.

- *We Shall Remain: After the Mayflower.* (2009) [Documentary]. Chris Eyre. Dir. USA: PBS.

ICONOGRAPHIC SOURCES

- *The Mayflower in Plymouth Harbor*, by William Formby Halsall, 1882. Royalty-free reproduction picture.

- Pocahontas saving John Smith's life, c. 1870. Royalty-free reproduction picture.

- Massasoit and John Carver smoking a peace pipe. Royalty-free reproduction picture.

- *Signing of the Mayflower Compact, 1620*, by Edward Percy Moran, c. 1900. Royalty-free reproduction picture.

- Mary Dyer being taken to the Boston Common to be hanged. Royalty-free reproduction picture.

- *Philip, King of Mount Hope*, by Paul Revere, 1772. Royalty-free reproduction picture.

Although the editor makes every effort to verify the accuracy of the information published, 50Minutes.com accepts no responsibility for the content of this book.

www.50minutes.com

Ebook EAN: 9782808002646

Paperback EAN: 9782808002653

Legal Deposit: D/2017/12603/653

Cover: © Primento

Digital conception by Primento, the digital partner of publishers.